D0801794

the pocket book of

COCKTAILS

the pocket book of
COCKTAILS

OVER 150 CLASSIC & CONTEMPORARY RECIPES

RYLAND PETERS & SMALL
LONDON • NEW YORK

Designer Paul Stradling
Editor Alice Sambrook
Production Controller Mai-Ling Collyer
Art Director Leslie Harrington
Editorial Director Julia Charles
Publisher Cindy Richards
Indexer Vanessa Bird

First published in 2016
This revised edition published in 2020
by Ryland Peters & Small
20–21 Jockey's Fields
London WC1R 4BW
and
341 E 116th St
New York NY 10029

www.rylandpeters.com

Text © Ben Reed, Carol Hilker, Janet Sawyer,
Shelagh Ryan, Ursula Ferrigno, Valerie Aikman-
Smith, William Yeoward and Ryland Peters &
Small 2016, 2020

Design and photographs © Ryland Peters &
Small 2016, 2020

ISBN: 978-1-78879-205-9

10 9 8 7 6 5 4 3 2 1

A CIP record for this book is available from the
British Library.
US Library of Congress Cataloging-in-Publication
data has been applied for.

Printed and bound in China

NOTES

Recipes make enough to serve 1 unless
stated in the individual introduction.

Measurements are occasionally given in
barspoons, which are equivalent to 5 ml or
1 teaspoon.

Ice cubes or crushed ice are not stated in
ingredients but are useful for most recipes.

All fruit and vegetables should be washed
thoroughly before consumption. Unwaxed citrus
fruits should be used whenever possible.

All eggs are large (US) or medium (UK), unless
specified as US extra-large, in which case UK
large should be used. Uncooked or partially
cooked eggs should not be served to the very
old, frail, young children, pregnant women or
those with compromised immune systems.

Both British (Metric) and American (Imperial
plus US cups) are included in these recipes for
your convenience; however, it is important to
work with one set of measurements and not
alternate between the two within a recipe.

CONTENTS

INTRODUCTION

The Pocket Book of Cocktails brings you over 150 recipes to choose from; never again will you find yourself without the perfect drink in hand. Whether you're hosting a sophisticated soirée, a tiki beach party, planning a festive get-together or simply indulging alone – a cocktail is one of the finest treats in life.

With this go-to guide for the aspiring mixologist, learn about essential tools, equipment and glassware, and become a fountain of cocktail knowledge to your friends and family by taking note of the little introduction to each drink.

Choose from the flirty sophistication of the **Vodka** chapter with a classic Cosmopolitan or Vodka Espresso. Try a grown-up classic from the **Gin** section such as the Negroni or Singapore Sling. Transport yourself to a sun-drenched beach bar with a **Rum**-based Piña Colada or Raspberry & Rose Mojito. Indulge in the old-fashioned wholesomeness of a **Whiskey** Mint Julep or Salted Caramel Bourbon Milkshake. Find fun and summery drinks like the Frozen Peach Margarita or Salty Dog in the **Tequila** section. Old favourites such as a Sidecar or Brandy Alexander are brought to the fore in **Brandy, Liqueurs & Aperitifs**. And for something really special flip to the **Champagne & Wine** section for a Limoncello Champagne or Al Fresco Bellini recipe.

Here you'll find a range of tasty beverages from revived vintage classics to modern and trendy creations. Get shaking, stirring and making – join the cocktail revolution!

EQUIPMENT

For the aspiring bartender, getting the right equipment can
be as important as the taste of the final drink itself. You will
probably find that you already have most of what you need to
make cocktails in your own kitchen. But if you want to create
the right atmosphere for your guests and mix cocktails with
a little more flair, it's worth getting a few accessories.

MEASURE/JIGGER

Measures/jiggers come in a variety of
sizes so you can pour the correct
quantity of drink. The dual measure is
a good choice, where one end holds
25 ml and the other holds 50 ml in the
UK, or 1 oz. and 2 oz. in the US.

SHAKER

Shake it up, baby! There are two basic
types of shaker: the three-piece (or
deco) shaker and the Boston shaker.
They come in all shapes and sizes,
from fire extinguishers to rockets.

MIXING GLASS

This is used for making drinks that are
stirred, not shaken.

BARSPOON

Handy for both stirring drinks and for
the gentle pouring required for layering

drinks. The flat end can be used for
muddling or crushing ingredients. The
barspoon holds around the same
amount of liquid as a regular teaspoon.

MUDDLER

A long pestle that's used for mixing or
crushing ingredients such as sugar
cubes, lemons or limes.

STRAINER

There are two types of strainer: the
Hawthorn strainer that will sit over
the metal part of the shaker, and the
Julep that fits comfortably in the
mixing glass.

STRAWS

A simple straw is a hygienic way to
test the taste of your tipple. Dip it into
the drink and place your finger over the
top end to create a vacuum. Take the

straw out and suck the liquid to see if it needs anything to be added.

BLENDER
To whizz up your drinks.

JUICER
Useful to extract the juice from fruits.

SWIZZLE STICKS
Used for stirring drinks. Plus it's rather fun to say.

QUALITY PARING KNIFE AND PEELER
A paring knife has a small sharp blade that makes it easier to complete fiddly or intricate jobs. A sharp peeler will make it much easier to prepare attractive garnishes.

GLASSWARE

When choosing the glass in which to serve your drink, first choose the appropriate size, eg. a highball for a long mixed drink, or an old-fashioned rocks glass for a short drink. The glassware used for a specific drink is designed to suit its composition – the Champagne glass is tall and thin to maintain the bubbles, the whiskey tumbler is squat to allow the drink's aroma to swirl around the glass. The following list of glasses should be all you need to show off your taste sensations. Remember, presentation is key!

SHOT GLASS (1)

Pretty self-explanatory, this small glass holds either a single or a double shot of liquor. Shooters (mixed layered shots such as the B52 p.149) are also served in these glasses.

TUMBLER (2)

Also known as an old-fashioned glass, rocks glass or lowball glass, a tumbler is used for short drinks over ice.

HIGHBALL GLASS (3)

This is a tall, thin glass used for serving long cocktails and summery drinks. Plenty of room for mixing fresh fruit and ice.

HEATPROOF GLASS (4)

A handled glass means you won't burn your fingers when slurping a hot toddy, mulled wine or Irish coffee. They are generally made of heat-resistant material that won't crack if filled with very hot liquid.

CHAMPAGNE FLUTE (5)

A tall, narrow glass that houses the bubbly stuff. Cheers!

WINE GLASS (6)

A glass that, er, holds wine. Some say the shape of a well-made wine glass can influence the flavour of the wine, so choose carefully.

MARTINI GLASS (7)

A must for any aspiring mixologist, this glass has a cone-shaped bowl atop a stem. Cocktails served in a martini glass should be chilled, and the long stem allows the drinker to hold it without affecting the temperature.

MARGARITA COUPETTE (8)

Similar to a martini glass but slightly larger and curved. Lovely for fruity or tropical cocktails.

HURRICANE GLASS (9)

Hold onto your hats! Also known as a tulip glass, this generally holds punches and frozen drinks. It's similarly shaped to a vase and is typically taller and wider than a highball glass.

JUG/PITCHER (NOT PICTURED)

A large container, usually with a handle and spout for pouring. Holds many servings so perfect for drinks like punch or Sangria.

VODKA

CLASSIC MARTINI pictured opposite

Perhaps the most iconic of all aperitifs, this elegant drink is perfect for any classy occasion. James Bond eat your heart out.

15 ml/½ oz. dry vermouth

75 ml/3 oz. vodka

twist of lemon zest

2 unstuffed green olives, to garnish

Pour the vermouth and vodka over ice in a mixing jug/pitcher. Stir to make the cocktail very cold. Strain into a martini glass. Hold the lemon zest over the glass and twist to spray a fine mist of its oils onto the cocktail. Discard the zest and garnish the martini with olives speared on a toothpick.

BREAKFAST MARTINI

Not recommended to accompany your cornflakes, unless early morning is actually last thing at night for you.

50 ml/2 oz. vodka

2 barspoons marmalade

Pour a large shot of vodka into a shaker filled with ice, add the marmalade, shake sharply and strain into a frosted martini glass.

APPLE MARTINI
pictured opposite

Vanilla and apple work beautifully together in this delicious
martini. Use the kooky sliced apple garnish pictured to jazz
up the slightly plain colour.

20 ml/⅔ oz. apple schnapps

40 ml/1½ oz. vanilla vodka

25 ml/1 oz. apple juice

2 barspoons fresh lime juice

2 barspoons sugar syrup
(page 91)

very thin slices of green-
and pink-skinned apple;
½ a vanilla pod/bean, to
garnish

Put all the ingredients into a cocktail shaker filled
with ice. Shake. Strain into a martini glass.
Garnish with the apple and vanilla. (If the apple
slices are freshly cut, they will 'stick' together in
a row.)

RASPBERRY MARTINI

This lovely pink drink should be quite thick in consistency;
it should flow down your throat like treacle.

50 ml/2 oz. vodka

a dash of framboise

a dash of orange bitters

15 ml/½ oz. raspberry purée

2 fresh raspberries, to
garnish

Shake all the ingredients in a shaker filled with
ice and strain into a pre-chilled martini glass.
Garnish with two raspberries.

FRENCH MARTINI pictured opposite

The French Martini is great for parties and simple to make in bulk. Shake hard when preparing and you will be rewarded with a thick white froth on the surface.

50 ml/2 oz. vodka

a large dash of Chambord (or crème de mure)

75 ml/3 oz. pineapple juice

Add all the ingredients to a shaker filled with ice, shake sharply and then strain into a frosted martini glass.

TURKISH CHOCOLATE MARTINI

This drink is pure indulgence. The heaviness of the crème de cacao combines with the lightness of the flower water to create a truly Turkish delight.

50 ml/2 oz. vodka

2 barspoons white crème de cacao

2 dashes of rose water

cocoa powder, for the glass

Add all the ingredients to a shaker filled with ice, shake well, then strain into a chilled martini glass edged with cocoa powder.

POLISH MARTINI
pictured opposite

The bitterness of Zubrowka and the potent sweetness of
Krupnik combine with the crispness of apple juice to create
a beguiling depth of taste.

25 ml/1 oz. Krupnik vodka

25 ml/1 oz. Zubrowka vodka

25 ml/1 oz. apple juice

Pour the two vodkas and the apple juice into a
mixing glass filled with ice. Stir and strain into
a chilled martini glass.

GOTHAM MARTINI

A cocktail that is as sinister and mysterious as its name
suggests. Try varying the amount of black Sambuca for a
darker, more thrilling result.

60 ml/2¼ oz. frozen
Stolichnaya vodka

a dash of black Sambuca

Pour the vodka into a chilled martini glass, gently
add the Sambuca, then serve.

COSMOPOLITAN pictured opposite

'Hi, I'd like a cheeseburger, please, large fries and a
Cosmopolitan' – Carrie Bradshaw. This sassy cocktail
is just as good with fancy nibbles as with fast food.

35 ml/1¼ oz. lemon vodka
20 ml/⅔ oz. triple sec
20 ml/⅔ oz. fresh lime juice
25 ml/1 oz. cranberry juice
lemon zest, to garnish

Add all the ingredients to a shaker filled with
ice, shake sharply and strain into a chilled
martini glass. Garnish with lemon zest for
that extra zing!

COSMO ROYALE

For a fizzy spin, add a float of Champagne. The bubbles will
happily sit on the surface if you pour them gently!

35 ml/1¼ oz. lemon vodka
15 ml/½ oz. fresh lime juice
15 ml/½ oz. Cointreau
25 ml/1 oz. cranberry juice
Champagne, to float
orange zest, to garnish

Add all the ingredients, except the Champagne,
to a shaker filled with ice. Shake sharply and
strain into a chilled martini glass. Float the
Champagne on the surface and garnish with
orange zest.

METROPOLITAN

pictured opposite

This cocktail is a fruity variation on the Cosmopolitan, using blackcurrant vodka, combined with cranberry and lime juices.

35 ml/1¼ oz. Absolut Kurant vodka or other blackcurrant-flavoured spirit

20 ml/⅔ oz. triple sec

20 ml/⅔ oz. fresh lime juice

25 ml/1 oz. cranberry juice

orange zest (flamed, if you like), to garnish

Shake all the ingredients sharply over ice and strain into a chilled martini glass.

To make a flaming orange zest, squeeze the oil from a strip of orange zest, held skin downwards and over a flame above the glass. Rub the rim with the orange zest before dropping it into the glass.

METROPOLIS

The Metropolis, inspired by the much-loved Kir Royale, features the addition to vodka of Champagne and berry-flavoured liqueur.

25 ml/1 oz. vodka

25 ml/1 oz. crème de framboise

Champagne, to top up

Shake the vodka and the crème de framboise together over ice and strain into a martini glass. Top with Champagne and serve.

SEA BREEZE pictured opposite

The Sea Breeze is a modern, thirst-quenching variation on the classic Screwdriver. The cranberry juice lends a light, fruity, refreshing quality and combines with the bitter grapefruit juice, making it very popular with people who don't particularly enjoy the taste of alcohol.

50 ml/2 oz. vodka
150 ml/⅔ cup cranberry juice
50 ml/2 oz. grapefruit juice
lime wedge, to garnish

Pour the vodka into a highball glass filled with ice. Three-quarters fill the glass with cranberry juice and top with fresh grapefruit juice. Garnish with a lime wedge and serve with two straws (optional).

HARVEY WALLBANGER

The story goes that Harvey, a Californian surfer who had performed particularly badly in an important contest, visited his local bar to drown his sorrows. He ordered his usual Screwdriver — only to decide that it wasn't strong enough for what he had in mind. Scanning the bar for something to boost his drink, his eyes fell on the distinctively shaped Galliano bottle, a shot of which was then added to his drink as a float.

50 ml/2 oz. vodka
15 ml/½ oz. Galliano
orange juice, to top up
orange slice, to garnish

Build the ingredients over ice into a highball glass, stir and serve with an orange slice.

BERRY CAIPIROSKA pictured opposite

When it's hot outside this delicious summery cocktail is perfectly refreshing. It can be made to taste with fresh berries of your choosing.

50 ml/2 oz. vodka

4 lime wedges

2 white sugar cubes

3 fresh berries, plus extra to garnish (strawberries, raspberries or blueberries)

Muddle all the ingredients in a rocks glass with a wooden pestle. Top up with crushed ice and stir gently to mix. Serve garnished with a few fresh berries skewered on a toothpick.

QUEEN OF TARTS pictured page 101, left

75 ml/3 oz. dry martini

50 ml/2 oz. vodka

freshly squeezed juice of ½ lemon

3 teaspoons caster/ granulated sugar

3 barspoons balsamic vinegar

6 strawberries, puréed

With its cheeky name and adventurous flavour, this balsamic strawberry temptress is perfect for serving at parties.

Combine all the ingredients and serve over ice in a martini glass.

LEGEND

Invented in London in the late 1980s by Dick Bradsell, this
recipe should be followed closely, as too much of any of the
ingredients can result in an unpalatable cocktail. Make sure
you taste each concoction before you serve it.

50 ml/2 oz. vodka

25 ml/1 oz. crème de mure

25 ml/1 oz. fresh lime juice

a dash sugar syrup (page 91)

lemon zest, to garnish
  (optional)

Add all the ingredients to a shaker filled with ice,
shake sharply and strain into a chilled martini
glass. Garnish with lemon zest.

MIX IT UP
Try replacing the crème de mure with your berry
liqueur of choice, such as a scrumptious crème de
fraise, crème de framboise or crème de cassis.

SILVER STREAK

Kummel is one of the least frequently used liqueurs in cocktails, more's the pity. It has a distinctive, almost aniseed-like taste that comes from the caraway seeds used in its production, and as an added bonus it promotes good digestion. For best results keep both the vodka and the kummel in a fridge or freezer and pour them gently into a sturdy old-fashioned glass for the perfect after-dinner nightcap.

25 ml/1 oz. chilled vodka

25 ml/1 oz. kummel

Pour a generous single measure of chilled vodka into a rocks glass filled with ice. Add a similar amount of kummel, stir gently and serve.

MIX IT UP

To inject some zesty zing into this simple drink, add 25 ml/1 oz. fresh lime juice and plenty of ice to the rest of the ingredients in a cocktail shaker. Shake well and strain into a chilled glass.

BLACK RUSSIAN

pictured opposite, left

Black and White Russians are classics that have been on the scene for many years. They make stylish after-dinner cocktails with their sweet coffee flavour, which is sharpened up by the vodka.

50 ml/2 oz. vodka

25 ml/1 oz. Kahlúa

stemmed cherry, to garnish

Shake the vodka and Kahlúa together over ice. Strain into a rocks glass filled with ice. Garnish with a stemmed cherry.

WHITE RUSSIAN

pictured opposite, right

The White Russian, with its addition of the cream float, is great served as a nightcap.

50 ml/2 oz. vodka

25 ml/1 oz. Kahlúa

25 ml/¾ oz. single/light cream

stemmed cherry, to garnish

To make a White Russian, make a Black Russian (see above) then layer the single cream into the glass over the back of a barspoon. As before, garnish with a stemmed cherry.

VODKA ESPRESSO

The dark and delicious Vodka Espresso is designed to awaken its recipient.

50 ml/2 oz. fresh espresso coffee

50 ml/2 oz. vodka

a dash of sugar syrup (page 91)

3 coffee beans, to garnish

Pour the espresso coffee into a shaker, add the vodka and sugar syrup to taste, shake the mixture sharply and strain into an old-fashioned glass filled with ice. Garnish with three coffee beans.

ALMOND VODKA ESPRESSO pictured opposite

A less-than-innocent concoction, composed of amaretto and vodka as well as a coffee liqueur. The amount of sugar you include in the espresso is up to you.

25 ml/1 oz. freshly made espresso, sweetened to taste

35 ml/1¼ oz. vodka

20 ml/⅔ oz. amaretto

15 ml/½ oz. Kahlúa or other coffee liqueur

3 coffee beans and a pinch of toasted, flaked/slivered almonds, to garnish

Pour all the ingredients into a shaker. Fill with ice and shake. Strain into a martini glass. Wait for the cocktail to 'separate' – a foam will rise to the top and the liquid below will become clearer. Garnish with the coffee beans and almonds.

BEST EVER BLOODY MARY

A Bloody Mary is the ultimate brunch drink, allowing you to ingest booze before midday with complete legitimacy. This recipe makes enough to serve 4 — a hangover shared is a hangover solved.

500 ml/2 cups tomato juice

400 g/2½ cups cherry tomatoes

30 ml/2 tablespoons Worcestershire sauce

30 ml/2 tablespoons Sriracha Chilli sauce

a 3-cm/1¼-inch piece of horseradish, finely grated

sea salt and freshly ground black pepper

60 ml/¼ cup fresh lime juice

300 ml/1¼ cups vodka

celery, to garnish

chilli/dried hot pepper flakes, to garnish

a food processor

Put the tomato juice and cherry tomatoes in a food processor and blend until smooth.

Transfer to a jug/pitcher and stir in the Worcestershire sauce, Sriracha chilli sauce and grated horseradish. Season with salt and pepper, cover with clingfilm/plastic wrap and chill in the fridge for at least 30 minutes.

When ready to serve, add the lime juice and vodka, and stir well. Place a pickled celery stick in 4 high-ball glasses, fill each glass with ice and pour in the Bloody Mary mixture. Garnish each with a pinch of chilli/dried red pepper flakes and enjoy!

MIX IT UP
For extra depth of flavour try roasting the cherry tomatoes before blending.

GIN

CLASSIC GIN MARTINI

pictured opposite

Stirring a martini to make the perfect mix is the original labour of love for any bartender. Add less vermouth for a 'dry' martini and more vermouth for a 'wet'.

a dash of vermouth

75 ml/3 oz. well-chilled gin

an olive or lemon twist, to garnish

Add both the ingredients to a mixing glass filled with ice and stir. Strain into a chilled martini glass and garnish with an olive or lemon twist.

SMOKY MARTINI

Adding a dash of smoky whiskey makes the martini an altogether different beast.

50 ml/2 oz. gin

a dash of dry vermouth

a dash of whisky

an olive, to garnish

Add the ingredients to a shaker filled with cracked ice. Shake sharply and strain into a frosted martini glass with a lemon-zested rim. Garnish with an olive.

TOKYO MARTINI

pictured opposite

This martini can be a bit intense if it is made without care.
Try to find the best-quality wasabi and the freshest ginger.

50 ml/2 oz. gin

2 thin strips of fresh ginger

a small roll of wasabi

ginger strip or slice,
  to garnish

Add the ingredients to a shaker filled with ice,
shake and strain into a frosted martini glass.
Garnish with a thin slice or strip of ginger.

SAPPHIRE MARTINI

A drizzle of Parfait Amour, a beautiful orange curaçao flavoured
with violets, combined with chilled Bombay Sapphire gin
produces a magnificent cocktail.

2 barspoons Parfait Amour

50 ml/2 oz. chilled Bombay
  Sapphire gin

fresh blueberries, to garnish

Gently pour the Parfait Amour into a chilled
martini glass. Pour the gin (which should have
been in the freezer for at least 1 hour) over a
barspoon, so that it sits over the liqueur. Garnish
with blueberries on a toothpick.

TOM COLLINS

Although many consider the Tom Collins to be an English drink, this early punch was actually first documented by Professor Jerry Thomas, the father of American cocktails, in 1876. It has remained a cocktail-party classic ever since.

50 ml/2 oz. gin

20 ml/⅔ oz. fresh lemon juice

15 ml/½ oz fresh fruit purée (pomegranate, raspberry and blueberry purées are all good)

sugar syrup, to taste (page 91)

soda water, to top up

seasonal fresh fruit, to garnish

Add all the ingredients except the soda water to a highball glass filled with ice and stir gently to mix. Top up with soda water and stir again. Garnish with seasonal fresh fruit.

MIX IT UP

The Tom Collins is a close relation of the Elderflower Collins. To make one of these, replace the fresh fruit purée with 15 ml/½ oz. elderflower cordial. Garnish with a slice of lemon and a sprig of fresh mint leaves. The botanicals in the gin get an unexpected boost from the elderflower, making this a delicate cocktail full of floral flavours.

SLOE GIN FIZZ pictured opposite

You may need to play around with the balance of flavours in this cocktail, as different brands of sloe gin have varying degrees of sweetness.

50 ml/2 oz. sloe gin

20 ml/⅔ oz. fresh lemon juice

a dash of sugar syrup (page 91)

soda water, to top up

lemon slice, to garnish

Add all the ingredients, except the soda, to a shaker filled with ice. Shake sharply and strain into a highball glass filled with ice.

Top with soda water, garnish with a lemon slice and serve with two straws (optional).

RAMOS GIN FIZZ

50 ml/2 oz. gin

25 ml/1 oz. single/light cream

20 ml/⅔ oz. egg white

20 ml/⅔ oz. fresh lemon juice

20 ml/⅔ oz. fresh lime juice

20 ml/⅔ oz. sugar syrup (page 91)

2 dashes of orange-flower water

a dash of soda water

Created by Henry Ramos, a saloon owner from New Orleans. Henry maintained that his Gin Fizz should be shaken for at least 5 minutes to achieve the right consistency. He even hired additional bartenders for this very purpose.

Add all the ingredients, except the soda, to a shaker filled with ice. Shake sharply for as long as you can, then shake some more.

Strain the fluffy mixture into a chilled Champagne flute, add a dash of soda water and serve.

NEGRONI

This is surely the Italian cocktail par excellence. Its flavour is
a splendid fusion of sweetness, spiciness and bitterness, giving
it a particular kind of 'strength' that might be considered to be
a reflection of Italian character. It is also deep and rich in
colour – an attractive drink all round.

25 ml/1 oz. Martini Rosso
vermouth

25 ml/1 oz. gin

25 ml/1 oz. Campari

orange wedges, to garnish

Fill an old-fashioned glass with ice. Pour in the
ingredients and gently stir. Garnish with the
orange wedges and serve with a swizzle stick.

MIX IT UP

If you prefer a taste that is less bitter, try a White
Negroni, made by replacing the vermouth with
Lillet Blanc and replacing the Campari with Suze.
Garnish with grapefruit or orange zest.

MARTINEZ

The Martinez is believed to be the first documented martini,
dating back as far as 1849. Its sweet flavours were geared
to appeal to the taste buds of the time and the availability
of certain spirits. This is a variation on a recipe from
Jerry Thomas.

50 ml/2 oz. Old Tom gin

15 ml/½ oz. sweet vermouth

a dash of orange bitters

a dash of maraschino liqueur

lemon twist, to garnish

Add all the ingredients to a shaker filled with ice,
shake and strain into a chilled martini glass.
Garnish with a lemon twist.

MIX IT UP

If you don't have maraschino, kirsch can be used
instead. This will produce a drink that is less
sweet. If you still want it sweet, add a dash of
sugar syrup (page 91).

GIN BRAMBLE pictured opposite

This is a perfect cocktail for drinking on a sunny deck in the cool of an early evening...blissful!

50 ml/2 oz. gin

25 ml/1 oz. fresh lemon juice

2 barspoons sugar syrup (page 91)

15 ml/½ oz. crème de mure

a lemon wedge and a blackberry, to garnish

Build the gin, lemon juice and sugar syrup over crushed ice in a rocks glass and stir. Drizzle the crème de mure over the ice and garnish with a lemon wedge and a fresh blackberry.

GIN GIMLET

Be sparing with the lime cordial, the Gimlet is among those drinks that can be ruined if the gin is drowned out.

50 ml/2 oz. gin

25 ml/1 oz. lime cordial

Pour the gin and cordial into a shaker filled with ice. Shake very sharply and strain into a frosted martini glass.

CLOVER CLUB

Invented around the turn of the last century, this drink was named after a group of high-fliers that would meet at the Bellevue-Stratford Hotel in Philadelphia. Try to use some raspberry syrup or make your own with fresh raspberries and sugar.

50 ml/2 oz. gin

20 ml/⅔ oz. fresh lemon juice

2 barspoons raspberry syrup

a dash of egg white

sugar syrup, to taste
  (page 91)

Add all the ingredients to a shaker filled with ice and shake sharply. Strain into a chilled cocktail glass.

MIX IT UP

A Royal Clover Club is a variation of the Clover Club that contains an egg yolk instead of egg white. This will slightly alter the texture and the colour to a rich orangey pink. Always make sure to use the best quality organic eggs in cocktails such as these.

GARRICK GIN PUNCH

If the dryness of a good London gin is your thing then this is your cocktail. Based on a 19th-century recipe from the exclusive Garrick Club in London, it makes a superb aperitif, cutting through the fug of your day and preparing your palate for whatever the evening holds. Shake it until it's as cold as can be and serve in a chilled glass.

50 ml/2 oz. London dry gin

25 ml/1 oz. fresh lemon juice

15 ml/½ oz. maraschino liqueur

a dash of sugar syrup (page 91)

2 dashes of Angostura bitters

lemon zest, to garnish

Add all the ingredients to a cocktail shaker filled with ice and shake together until the outside of the shaker starts to frost.

Strain into a frosted coupette glass and serve garnished with a thin piece of lemon zest.

MIX IT UP

Fresh lime juice works well in place of the lemon juice and adds a pleasing green tinge to the drink.

SINGAPORE SLING

Created in the early 1900s at the Long Bar at the Raffles hotel in Singapore, when this drink is made correctly — and without using one of the cheap pre-mixes that are so prevalent today — it is the peak of sophistication! The original recipe has long been a subject of hot debate; this is one of the best.

25 ml/1 oz. gin

25 ml/1 oz. cherry brandy

1 barspoon Benedictine

25 ml/1 oz. fresh lemon juice

a small dash of Angostura bitters

soda water, to top up

lemon zest curls and cocktail cherries, to garnish

Put all the ingredients in a small pitcher/jug filled with ice and stir gently to mix. Top up with soda water.

Serve in a tall, ice-filled glass, garnished with a lemon zest curl and a cocktail cherry.

MIX IT UP
If this cocktail tickles your fancy then you could also try the Chinatown Sling. Simply replace the lemon juice with pineapple juice and garnish with cocktail cherries and a pineapple triangle.

WATERMELON GIN

The summery flavour of ripe red watermelon goes wonderfully well with the fresh, clean, lemony taste of gin. The seed-free section in the middle of a melon is the sweetest, so if you're cutting pieces for a garnish use this part.

½ very ripe watermelon, well chilled

50 ml/2 oz. gin (or to taste)

sprigs of fresh mint, to garnish

a food processor

Cut the watermelon in half and remove the rind and seeds. Whizz the flesh in a food processor. If the mixture is too thick, add water.

Pour into a jug/pitcher, stir in the gin and serve in small glasses with plenty of crushed ice and a sprig of mint.

MIX IT UP

Cantaloupe melon can be used in place of watermelon – due to its firmer texture, whizz for slightly longer in the food processor. Lovely with a dash of elderflower liqueur.

WHITE LADY WITH VANILLA

Vanilla is a modern addition to the classic version of a White Lady; it helps to round out and deepen the flavour. This is a classy and delicious cocktail, perfect for any ladies who lunch — or men, for that matter.

50 ml/2 oz. gin

15 ml/½ oz. fresh lemon juice

15 ml/½ oz. Cointreau

½ a vanilla pod/bean

Put the gin, lemon juice, Cointreau and vanilla pod/bean (split if you'd like the seeds to add extra vanilla flavour to your cocktail) into a cocktail shaker with a few ice cubes.

Shake very well with ice, remove the vanilla pod/bean, and serve in a cocktail glass.

MIX IT UP

To enhance your cocktail why not split a vanilla pod/bean and put it in a jar of sugar for two weeks or more, then use the sugar on the rim of your cocktail glass. Wet the rim of your glass with lemon juice and then dip into the sugar.

WHISKEY

MINT JULEP

First consumed in the late 1700s, the granddaddy of cocktails was traditionally served on Kentucky Derby Day. These days it's a cocktail for the more discerning amongst us.

15 ml/½ oz. sugar syrup (page 91)

3 fresh mint sprigs

60 ml/2¼ oz. bourbon

Muddle the sugar syrup, one mint sprig and the bourbon in a rocks glass. Add crushed ice and garnish with the remaining mint sprigs. Serve with two straws (optional).

MIX IT UP

For a different take on this classic, use brandy instead of bourbon to create a Brandy Mint Julep.

SWEET MANHATTAN pictured opposite

For those with a sweet tooth, the addition of orange bitters provides a subtle shift in flavour to this classic drink.

50 ml/2 oz. rye whiskey

25 ml/1 oz. sweet vermouth

a dash of orange bitters

maraschino cherry,
  to garnish

Add the ingredients to a mixing glass filled with ice (first ensure all the ingredients are very cold) and stir the mixture until chilled. Strain into a frosted martini glass, add the garnish and serve.

PERFECT MANHATTAN

'Perfect' does not refer to how well the drink is put together, it describes the perfect balance between sweet and dry.

50 ml/2 oz. rye whiskey

15 ml/½ oz. sweet vermouth

15 ml/½ oz. dry vermouth

a dash of Angostura bitters

orange zest, to garnish

Add the ingredients to a mixing glass filled with ice (first ensure all the ingredients are very cold) and stir the mixture until chilled. Strain into a frosted martini glass, add the garnish and serve.

ROB ROY pictured opposite

Have fun choosing from the vast range of whiskies available to star in this cocktail.

50 ml/2 oz. Scotch whisky

20 ml/⅔ oz. sweet vermouth

a dash of Angostura bitters

lemon zest, to garnish

Add all the ingredients to a mixing glass filled with ice and stir gently with a barspoon. Strain into a chilled rocks glass filled with ice and garnish with a thin piece of lemon zest.

CARAMEL ROB ROY

Judging by the name of this cocktail, there can't be much doubt that we shall be having a 'wee dram'. What a treat this becomes with the caramel syrup.

2 barspoons Antica Formula vermouth

2 barspoons Noilly Prat dry vermouth

2 barspoons caramel syrup

50 ml/2 oz. Bowmore 12-year-old malt whisky

6 drops of orange bitters

orange twist, to garnish

Pour all the ingredients into a shaker or mixing jug. Add ice and stir vigorously. Double-strain into a coupe glass. Mist with the orange twist. Run the twist around the rim of the glass, then drop it gently into the cocktail.

OLD FASHIONED

pictured opposite

During the Prohibition era, strong flavourings such as
Angostura bitters were used in cocktails to disguise the
taste of illegally produced spirits, or 'moonshine'.

1 sugar cube

2 dashes of Angostura bitters

50 ml/2 oz. rye whiskey or
bourbon

orange zest, to garnish

Muddle all the ingredients in a rocks glass,
adding ice as you go. Garnish with orange zest
and serve.

WALNUT & MAPLE OLD FASHIONED

This is a cocktail that comes into its own in the fall/autumn,
when the inclusion of nuts is especially fitting.

2 half-slices orange

2 barspoons maple syrup

2 barspoons walnut syrup

6 drops of orange bitters

60 ml/2 oz. walnut-infused
bourbon whiskey

orange zest, to garnish

Muddle the orange in an old-fashioned glass.
Add the rest of the ingredients and fill with ice
cubes. Stir slowly for a minute or so to allow the
ice to dilute the bourbon slightly and for the
flavours to develop. Garnish with the orange zest.

WHISKEY SAZERAC

One of the earliest recorded cocktails, the Sazerac probably came into this world in the 1850s. It was originally made with brandy, but works really well with rye whiskey too. The rinse of absinthe adds an intricate layer of complexity to the drink.

50 ml/2 oz. rye whiskey

2 barspoons sugar syrup (page 91)

2 dashes of Peychaud's bitters

2 barspoons absinthe, to rinse the glass

thin lemon zest, to garnish

Stir all the ingredients, except the absinthe, in a mixing glass filled with ice. Rinse a chilled rocks glass with the absinthe. Strain the contents of the mixing glass into the rocks glass and garnish with a thin zest of lemon.

MIX IT UP

Instead of using sugar syrup, muddle a brown sugar cube with a little water and the rye whiskey, before straining into the absinthe rinsed glass. A bit more time consuming, but this will add a richness to the flavour of the cocktail.

WHISKEY MAC
pictured opposite, left

**For people who like their drinks spicy but not too sweet.
For a weaker version, serve in a long glass and top up
with ginger ale or ginger beer.**

50 ml/2 oz. whiskey

50 ml/2 oz. green ginger wine

a twist of lemon zest

ginger ale or ginger beer
  (optional)

Shake the whiskey, ginger wine and ice cubes in a cocktail shaker. Strain into a small glass and serve with a twist of lemon zest.

WHISKEY SOUR
pictured opposite, right

**Probably the most popular of all sour drinks, this is one
sophisticated tipple.**

freshly squeezed juice of
  1 lemon

2½ barspoons sugar syrup
  (page 91)

50 ml/2 oz. bourbon whiskey

a few drops Angostura
  bitters (optional)

lemon zest, to garnish

Add the lemon juice, sugar syrup, bourbon whiskey and Angostura bitters to the shaker and shake. Pour into a rocks glass filled with ice. Garnish with the lemon zest.

BOSTON SOUR

pictured opposite

A variation on the Whiskey Sour (page 72) with the addition of
an egg white. Scotch or bourbon will work but bourbon brings
a vanillary sweetness that is fantastic.

50 ml/2 oz. bourbon

25 ml/1 oz. fresh lemon juice

2 barspoons sugar syrup
(page 91)

2 dashes of Angostura bitters

a dash of egg white

lemon slice and maraschino
cherry, to garnish

Add all the ingredients to a shaker filled with ice
and shake sharply. Strain the contents into a
rocks glass filled with ice, and garnish with a
lemon slice and a maraschino cherry.

BOURBON COBBLER

For a deliciously tropical alternative to a Mint Julep (page 63),
try a refreshing Bourbon Cobbler. Gently ease the juice out of
the fruit for a sharp citrus flavour.

a pineapple slice

an orange slice

a lemon slice

50 ml/2 oz. bourbon

15 ml/½ oz. orange curaçao

a fresh mint sprig, to garnish

Gently muddle the fruit in a rocks glass. Add the
bourbon, curaçao and ice and stir well. Add more
ice and stir again. Garnish with a sprig of fresh
mint and serve with two short straws (optional).

KENTUCKY

If you are mad about both whiskey and passion fruit you will adore this cocktail. The fruit and mint not only bring a delicious freshness to the drink, but also balance the warmth of the Jack Daniel's.

5 fresh mint leaves

15 ml/½ oz. passion fruit purée

1 passion fruit

25 ml/1 oz. apple juice

15 ml/½ oz. sugar syrup (page 91)

50 ml/2 oz. Jack Daniel's single barrel whiskey

½ passion fruit and a fresh mint sprig, to garnish

Muddle the mint with the passion fruit purée in a shaker. Halve the passion fruit and scoop the pulp into the shaker, add the remaining ingredients, and top up with ice. Shake. Double-strain into a martini glass, then garnish with the passion fruit and mint.

MIX IT UP

Try a pomegranate purée (strained) instead of the passion fruit purée. Garnish with a few beautiful pomegranate seeds.

LYNCHBURG LEMONADE

You may find variations of this recipe using triple sec or
Cointreau as the sweetening agent. This version uses sugar
for its coarseness and fresh lemon wedges muddled together
for a more 'rustic' feel.

2 lemon wedges

2 barspoons caster/
  granulated sugar

50 ml/2 oz. Jack Daniel's

lemonade, to top up

Muddle the lemon and sugar together in a
highball glass. Add ice and the remaining
ingredients. Stir gently and serve with two
straws (optional).

MIX IT UP

Replace the caster/granulated sugar with
2 barspoons of grenadine syrup to make a
Pink Lynchburg Lemonade that is pretty as
a picture. Garnish with fresh mint leaves for
that extra flourish.

HOT TODDY

For some reason this drink is often only consumed when the drinker feels under the weather — but the Hot Toddy is some people's winter warmer of choice. It's perfect for sipping after any outdoor activity when things have turned frosty.

50 ml/2 oz. Scotch whisky

20 ml/⅔ dark honey

25 ml/1 oz. fresh lemon juice

a pinch of ground cinnamon or 1 cinnamon stick

boiling water, to top up

2 pieces of lemon zest, studded with cloves, to garnish

Add all the ingredients to a heatproof glass or pewter tankard and stir gently to mix. Top up with boiling water and serve garnished with a piece of lemon zest studded with cloves.

MIX IT UP

A Hot Ginger Toddy is a wonderful variation to try because ginger is the perfect complement to whiskey. Just add 15 ml/½ oz. ginger liqueur in place of the cinnamon and cloves.

BLUE BLAZER pictured opposite

A spectacular drink, but one that is best practised in the safe confines of the kitchen before trying it in front of an audience.

1 sugar cube

50 ml/2 oz. boiling water

50 ml/2 oz. whiskey

grated nutmeg, to garnish

Warm two small metal tankards. In one, dissolve the sugar in the boiling water. Pour the whiskey into the other. Set the whiskey alight and, as it burns, pour the liquid into the first tumbler and back, from one to another, creating a continuous stream of fire.

Once the flame has died down, pour the mixture into a warmed old-fashioned glass and garnish with a sprinkling of grated nutmeg.

RUSTY NAIL

This one's purely for the colder months, ideally when you are curled up in front of an open fire with a good book.

30 ml/1¼ oz. whiskey

30 ml/1¼ oz. Drambuie

orange zest, to garnish

Add both ingredients to a glass filled with ice and muddle with a barspoon. Garnish with orange zest.

SALTED CARAMEL BOURBON MILKSHAKE

This adults-only milkshake combines the best of both worlds, milkshake and bourbon. The recipe serves 4 people – it's simply too good to keep to yourself.

1 litre/4 cups salted caramel ice cream

250 ml/1 cup chocolate milk

1 teaspoon sea salt

150 ml/⅔ cup bourbon

a blender

Blend the ice cream, chocolate milk, sea salt and bourbon in a blender, adding ice depending on how thick you want your shake. Pour into lowball glasses or tumblers.

MIX IT UP

Try using good quality chocolate ice cream instead of salted caramel for an intensely chocolatey hit. Add a sprinkle of grated chocolate or a topping of whipped cream and caramel sauce for even more indulgence.

RUM

MOJITO pictured opposite

The Mojito has had a big revival on the cocktail scene. Here is the classic recipe.

2 lime wedges

2 barspoons caster/
  granulated sugar

9 fresh mint sprigs

50 ml/2 oz. light rum

a dash of soda water

sugar syrup, to taste
  (page 91)

Muddle the lime, sugar and mint (reserving a sprig for the garnish) in the bottom of a highball glass. Fill with plenty of crushed ice and add the rum. Stir well and add a dash of soda water. Add a dash or two of sugar syrup, to taste. Garnish with the mint sprig and serve.

RASPBERRY & ROSE MOJITO

This raspberry-and-rose Mojito makes for a delicate and enchanting cocktail.

15 ml/½ oz. rose syrup

8 fresh mint leaves

50 ml/2 oz. light rum

freshly squeezed juice of
  1 lime

15 ml/½ oz. crème de
  framboise

2 rose petals and a fresh
  mint sprig, to garnish

Pour the rose syrup into a highball glass. Add the mint leaves and rum. Delicately press the mint with the back of a barspoon. Add the lime juice and enough ice to come two-thirds of the way up the glass. Gently churn with the spoon. Pile up with more crushed ice and drizzle over the crème de framboise. Garnish with rose petals and mint.

ORIGINAL DAIQUIRI

This classic cocktail was made famous at the El Floridita restaurant, Havana, early in the 20th century. Experiment to find your perfect balance of golden rum, sharp citrus juice and sweet sugar syrup.

50 ml/2 oz. golden rum

20 ml/⅔ oz. fresh lime juice

2 barspoons sugar syrup
(page 91)

Pour all the ingredients into an ice-filled shaker. Shake and strain into a chilled martini glass.

ORANGE DAIQUIRI pictured opposite

The Orange Daiquiri substitutes the sweet Martinique rum called Creole Shrub for the Cuban rum of the Original Daiquiri, so uses a little less sugar syrup.

50 ml/2 oz. Creole Shrub rum

20 ml/⅔ oz. fresh lime juice

1 barspoon sugar syrup
(page 91)

Pour all the ingredients into an ice-filled shaker. Shake and strain into a chilled martini glass.

THE LOUNGER

The title of this cocktail incorporates the names of the ingredients, rather than referring to your likely activities after you've drunk a few, by the way. It will work nicely with light or dark rum.

25 ml/1 oz. fresh lime juice

25 ml/1 oz. vanilla-infused rum

25 ml/1 oz. ginger cordial

¼ teaspoon sugar syrup (see method)

1 glacé/candied cherry, to garnish

To make the sugar syrup, put 2 parts caster/granulated sugar to 1 part water in a saucepan (the quantities depend, of course, on how much sugar syrup you want to make), and boil until the sugar has just dissolved. Leave to cool completely before using.

Measure the lime, rum, ginger and sugar syrup into a cocktail shaker. Add a couple of ice cubes, replace the lid and shake hard. Pour into a cocktail glass and add a glacé/candied cherry if you want a touch of extra sweetness.

MIX IT UP

Golden rum can be infused with all manner of delicious delicacies. Make your own spiced rum by popping a cinnamon stick, cloves, star anise and orange zest into a bottle of golden rum and leaving to impart flavour for at least 24 hours.

BACARDI COCKTAIL

One of the best-known Daiquiri variations and one that must be made with the Bacardi brand of white rum, as decreed by a New York court action in 1936.

50 ml/2 oz. Bacardi white rum

3 barspoons grenadine

20 ml/⅔ oz. fresh lime juice

Shake all the ingredients sharply over ice, then strain into a chilled martini glass and serve.

MIX IT UP

Try making a Sour Bacardi Cocktail by replacing the grenadine with a sour mix syrup and the lime juice with apple juice. The luminous green colour will be quite the opposite of the pink drink pictured right.

HURRICANE pictured opposite

This cocktail was created by Pat O'Brien in his New Orleans tavern in the 1940s. Try to use proper passion fruit syrup instead of ready-made hurricane mix.

50 ml/2 oz. dark rum

25 ml/1 oz. fresh lemon juice

25 ml/1 oz. passion fruit syrup

passion fruit juice (optional)

passion fruit seeds,
  to garnish

Add all the ingredients to a cocktail shaker filled with ice and shake vigorously to mix.

Strain into a hurricane glass or tiki mug filled with crushed ice, top up with passion fruit juice, if using, and serve garnished with passion fruit seeds.

BAY BREEZE

An uncomplicated and refreshing cocktail, but don't be fooled into thinking this one tastes better with vodka.

50 ml/2 oz. golden rum

100 ml/4 oz. cranberry juice

50 ml/2 oz. pineapple juice

lime wedge, to garnish

Add all the ingredients to a shaker filled with ice, shake and strain into a highball glass filled with ice. Garnish with a lime wedge.

CUBA LIBRE _{pictured opposite}

One of the most famous of all rum-based drinks, reputed to have been invented by an army officer in Cuba shortly after Coca Cola was first produced in the 1890s.

50 ml/2 oz. white rum

1 lime

cola, to top up

Pour the rum into a highball glass filled with ice. Cut a lime into eighths, squeeze and drop the wedges into the glass. Top with cola and serve with straws (optional).

GINGER RUM

Rum and ginger are a marriage made in heaven – the very essence of the tropics! Golden rum from Barbados is a great compromise between the elegance of white rum and the power-flavour of dark rum. This can be served as a short cocktail or as a long drink with your favourite mixer.

1 piece stem ginger, crushed to a purée with a fork

1 barspoon ginger syrup from the jar

60 ml/2¼ oz. golden rum

15 ml/½ oz. fresh lime juice

lime wedge, to garnish

Put the puréed stem ginger, ginger syrup, rum and lime juice into a shaker filled with ice. Shake well, then strain into a glass filled with ice and garnish with a wedge of lime. Add extra syrup if you prefer a sweeter drink. Alternatively, whizz in a blender, then strain over ice.

For a long drink, serve in a Collins glass topped with ginger ale or soda.

PIÑA COLADA

A sweet, creamy drink that, for a time, epitomized the kind of cocktail that 'real' cocktail drinkers disapproved of (compare the somewhat ostentatious Piña Colada with a simple Dry Martini). However, since its creation in the 1970s, it has won widespread popularity, and now that we are in the new millennium, cocktails are for everyone so there's no shame in ordering a Piña Colada at the bar.

50 ml/2 oz. golden rum
25 ml/1 oz. coconut cream
15 ml/½ oz. single/light cream
25 ml/1 oz. pineapple juice

a blender

Put all the ingredients into a blender, add a scoop of crushed ice and blend. Pour into a sour or collins glass and garnish with a thick slice of pineapple.

MIX IT UP
Be warned, this variation is only for the very sweet toothed! For a Honey Colada (pictured opposite, left), add 2 barspoons of honey or sugar syrup to the glass after the drink has been poured. A sweet surprise will be left lurking at the bottom of the glass.

MON CHERI pictured opposite, right*

Vinegar-based cocktails are a fashionable favourite on the London cocktail circuit and rightly so. The vinegar cuts through the sweetness of the cocktail, adding a delicious sweet and sour flavour. You may have difficulty stopping at one glass! This one is for all those chocolate and cherry lovers out there.

50 ml/2 oz. Grand Marnier

25 ml/1 oz. rum

2 tablespoons finely grated dark/bittersweet chocolate

15 ml/½ oz. cherry liqueur

2 barspoons cider vinegar

Shake all the ingredients together and serve with ice.

MIX IT UP
If you fancy this cocktail without the sour edge of the cider vinegar, replace it with 2 barspoons of chocolate liqueur. It will taste like black forest gâteau in a glass.

*pictured opposite, left: Queen of Tarts – see page 26 for recipe

DARK & STORMY pictured opposite

The Dark & Stormy is hailed as the national drink of Bermuda. Although its name sounds like trouble it is refreshing served over ice. Homemade ginger beer gives this drink a zestier flavour.

60 ml/2¼ oz. Goslings Black Seal rum or similar

ginger beer, to top up

lime wedges, to serve

Fill a chilled glass with crushed ice. Pour in the rum and top with ginger beer. Finish with a squeeze of lime and serve.

DARK & STRAWMY

Adding fresh strawberries to this cocktail lightens some of the heavier rum flavours and makes the drink a little sweeter.

3 lime slices

2 strawberries, sliced, plus extra to garnish

50 ml/2 oz. dark rum

ginger beer, to top up

Muddle the lime and the strawberries in a highball glass. Add ice and the remaining ingredients and stir gently. Serve with a straw (optional) and half a strawberry to garnish.

BALTIMORE EGGNOG
pictured opposite

25 ml/1 oz. Madeira wine

15 ml/½ oz. Cognac

15 ml/½ oz. Jamaican rum

a pinch of ground cinnamon

1 tablespoon caster/
granulated sugar

1 egg

25 ml/1 oz. double/heavy
cream

grated nutmeg, to garnish

In essence, eggnog is a mixture of cream (or milk), sugar and beaten egg that can have alcohol added to it. Of the many variations around, Baltimore Eggnog is possibly the best: three different types of liquor as well as the dusting of spice really add extra depth.

Add all the ingredients to a cocktail shaker and shake vigorously for 15 seconds. Pour into a glass, grate over a little nutmeg and serve.

HOT BUTTERED RUM

Rum may be the perfect ingredient for a summer Caribbean-style cocktail, but it also lends itself to those winter nights, when combined with the spices and the brown sugar. Try also adding cinnamon or vanilla to the mix for added complexity.

3 teaspoons brown sugar

50 ml/2 oz. dark rum

½ teaspoon allspice

1 teaspoon butter

hot water, to top up

orange zest studded with
cloves, to garnish

Warm a heat-resistant glass and add the sugar and a little hot water. Stir until the sugar has dissolved and then add the rum, allspice and butter. Top up with hot water and stir until the butter has melted.

Garnish with a piece of orange zest studded with cloves and serve.

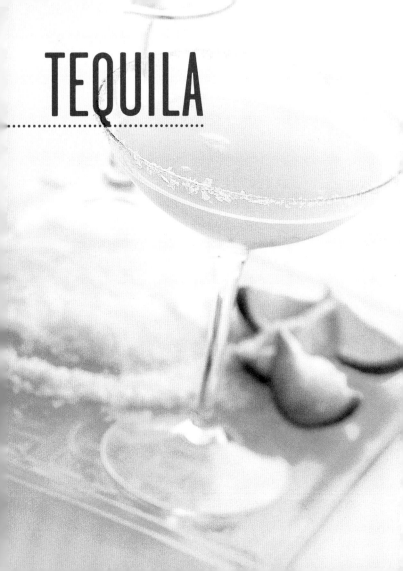

TEQUILA

CLASSIC MARGARITA pictured opposite

Treat this cool cocktail with the respect it deserves. Stay away from premixes, too much ice and cordial. Instead use fresh lemon or lime and gold tequila, which usually has a smoother taste than silver.

50 ml/2 oz. gold tequila

25 ml/1 oz. triple sec or Cointreau

freshly squeezed juice of ½ lime

salt, for the glass

Shake all the ingredients sharply with crushed ice then strain into a frosted margarita glass rimmed with salt.

LAHARA MARGARITA

Named after the oranges grown on the island of Curaçao, the Lahara fruit is inedibly bitter – it is the zest that is used to flavour the blue curaçao.

50 ml/2 oz. reposado tequila

20 ml/⅔ oz. blue curaçao

20 ml/⅔ oz. triple sec

freshly squeezed juice of ½ lime

Add all the ingredients to a shaker filled with crushed ice. Shake and then strain into a frosted margarita glass or punch cup.

FROZEN PEACH MARGARITA

The Frozen Peach Margarita is a real crowd pleaser on a warm day. It can be made in season when peaches are ripe and juicy, but frozen peaches are best if you want to create an ice-cold, frozen drink. The chilli/chili salt adds a taste of Mexico.

¼ teaspoon chipotle chilli/
  chili powder

1 tablespoon sea salt flakes

50 ml/2 oz. tequila

25 ml/1 oz. peach schnapps

225 g/½ lb. frozen peaches

finely grated zest and freshly
  squeezed juice of 1 lime

a blender

Mix together the chilli/chili powder and salt flakes. Wet the rim of a glass with the squeezed lime and dip into the chilli/chili salt. Set aside.

Put the remaining ingredients in a blender and blend until smooth. Serve in the salted glass.

MIX IT UP

When it comes to frozen Margaritas, the world of fruit is your oyster! Blood orange, pear, strawberry, kiwi, pineapple; any fruit with soft and tender flesh will work. Don't forget to replace the peach schnapps with the corresponding flavour. You could also try a Frozen Coconut Margarita variation using coconut cream for a gorgeous rich and creamy finish.

MANGORITA
pictured opposite

This cocktail is an easy one to make, but can be tricky to get right — mango is a powerfully flavoured fruit but you still need to be able to taste the tequila.

50 ml/2 oz. gold tequila

20 ml/⅔ oz. triple sec

20 ml/⅔ oz. fresh lime juice

25 ml/1 oz. mango purée
(or ¼ peeled mango)

mango slice, to garnish

a blender

Add all the ingredients to a blender. Add two scoops of crushed ice and blend for 20 seconds. Pour into a margarita coupette and garnish with a slice of mango.

PIÑARITA

The combination of pineapple and tequila results in a truly tropical flavour. This one deserves to be decorated lavishly.

50 ml/2 oz. gold tequila

20 ml/⅔ oz. triple sec

20 ml/⅔ oz. fresh lime juice

25 ml/1 oz. pineapple juice

pineapple slice, to garnish

a blender

Add all the ingredients to a blender. Add two scoops of crushed ice and blend for 20 seconds. Pour into a hurricane glass, garnish with a pineapple slice and serve with a couple of straws (optional).

LAGERITA

This is a tequila-based drink for the more adventurous among us. It is essential that a dark lager is used.

1 lime

25 ml/1 oz. gold tequila

1 brown sugar cube

Dark lager beer, such as
  Modelo Negra, to top up

Cut the lime into quarters, squeeze and drop them into a highball glass. Add the tequila and the sugar cube and muddle using a barspoon. Fill the glass with ice and add the beer.

Muddle again, ensuring as much of the sugar as possible has dissolved. Serve with two straws (optional).

MIX IT UP

Not a beer drinker? Try a Ciderita. Cider will be sweet enough to hold its own in this cocktail, so omit the sugar cube and combine the tequila and lime with a cider of your choice, muddling together as in the recipe above. Garnish the glass with apple slices.

SALTY CHIHUAHUA pictured opposite

A variation on the classic Salty Dog, which uses gin or vodka,
this cocktail is a recommended morning-after fix. A simple
combination that can cut through the fog of any hangover.

50 ml/2 oz. gold tequila

200 ml/8 oz. grapefruit juice

lime wedge, to garnish

salt, for the rim

Pour the tequila into a salt-rimmed highball
glass filled with ice. Top with grapefruit juice,
garnish with a lime wedge and serve with two
straws (optional).

SWEET CHIHUAHUA

A sweet and refreshing variation of the recipe above. The sugar
on the rim of the glass is delicious with the sour grapefruit.

50 ml/2 oz. tequila

a dash of hibiscus cordial

200 ml/8 oz. grapefruit juice

lime wedge, to garnish

sugar, for the rim

Pour the tequila and hibiscus cordial into a
sugar-edged highball glass filled with ice. Top
with the grapefruit juice, garnish with a lime
wedge and serve.

DIABLO pictured opposite

The Diablo is a long and refreshing classic cocktail that dates back to the 1940s. The spice of the ginger is soothed by the delicate hint of blackcurrant and invigorated by the fresh lime.

50 ml/2 oz. gold tequila
15 ml/½ oz. fresh lime juice
15 ml/½ oz. crème de cassis
ginger ale, to top up
redcurrants, to garnish

Build all the ingredients in a hurricane glass filled with crushed ice. Garnish with a small bunch of redcurrants and a devil fork swizzle stick.

TRES COMPADRES

50 ml/2 oz. gold tequila
20 ml/⅔ oz. Cointreau
20 ml/⅔ oz. Chambord
25 ml/1 oz. fresh lime juice
20 ml/⅔ oz. orange juice
20 ml/⅔ oz. grapefruit juice
lime wedge, to garnish
salt, for the glass

The combination of lime, orange and grapefruit juice provide the three citrus compadres. Cointreau and Chambord are then added to the mix to sweeten, and lo and behold, a great cocktail is born. Try serving this long (by adding more orange and grapefruit juice) for an extra-refreshing cooler.

Add all the ingredients to a shaker filled with ice. Shake sharply and strain into a chilled margarita glass edged with salt. Garnish with a lime wedge.

GREEN IGUANA _{pictured opposite}

The combination of melon and tequila works perfectly here. Midori (a melon-flavoured liqueur) is used in this recipe as fresh melon is not quite sweet enough.

50 ml/2 oz. Sauza Hornitos tequila

25 ml/1 oz. Midori

25 ml/1 oz. fresh lime juice

Add all the ingredients to a shaker filled with ice. Shake sharply and strain into a rocks glass filled with ice.

HORNY TOAD

Made using Sauza Hornitos tequila, the Horny Toad is named after the creature used to exemplify ugliness in Mexico. Strangely enough, you may find everyone much more attractive after drinking this!

35 ml/1¼ oz. Sauza Hornitos tequila

25 ml/1 oz. Cointreau

40 ml/1½ oz. fresh lime or lemon juice

salt, for the glass

Add all the ingredients to a shaker filled with ice. Shake sharply and strain into an ice-filled margarita glass, rimmed with salt.

PALOMA PUNCH
pictured opposite

Where possible, use fresh grapefruit juice for this cocktail. This recipe will make enough punch to serve 10 people. Party time!

500 ml/2 cups reposado tequila

100 ml/⅓ cup agave syrup

1.5 litres/6 cups grapefruit juice

3 limes

soda water, to top up

salt, for the glasses

Put the tequila, agave syrup, and grapefruit juice in a jug/pitcher filled with ice. Squeeze the limes into the pitcher and drop the husks in too, reserving one for preparing the glasses. Top up with the soda water and stir gently to mix.

To prepare the glasses, pour some salt onto a plate. Rub the rim of the glasses with the spent lime husk. Turn each glass upside down and place it in the salt so that it coats the rim.

Fill the salt-rimmed glasses with ice, top up with punch and serve.

RED CACTUS

50 ml/2 oz. Sauza Extra Gold tequila

20 ml/⅔ oz. triple sec

20 ml/⅔ oz. Chambord

35 ml/1¼ oz. fresh lime juice

4 fresh raspberries

lime slices, to garnish

a blender

The fresh raspberries and Chambord in this drink provide a fruity punch that almost masks the flavour of its base spirit. Don't be deceived; there's still plenty of tequila.

Add all the ingredients to a blender. Add two scoops of crushed ice and blend for 20 seconds.

Pour into a margarita coupette or hurricane glass. Garnish with lime slices and serve immediately.

SILK STOCKING

This tequila drink was invented during the 1920s in the US, at a time when cocktails were often given names revelling in innuendo and sensuality.

35 ml/1¼ oz. gold tequila

15 ml/½ oz. white crème de cacao

15 ml/½ oz. grenadine

15 ml/½ oz. double/heavy cream

2 fresh raspberries, to garnish

a blender

Add all the ingredients to a blender. Add two scoops of crushed ice and blend for 20 seconds. Pour the mixture into a hurricane glass, garnish with two raspberries and serve with two straws (optional).

MIX IT UP

Take away the grenadine and you are left with a snowy white 'Frostbite' cocktail. Alternatively, add a delicate dash of blue curaçao instead of the grenadine and you will be left with a baby blue 'Satin Stocking'.

BRANDY, LIQUEURS & APERITIFS

HORSE'S NECK

When you are dealing with strong flavours such as bitters,
you have to be cautious about the amount of drops or dashes
you use in a cocktail. It's all a question of getting the balance
right. The Horse's Neck, which has been highly popular since
the 1930s, is a finely balanced example of a classic cocktail
that first appeared, in the States, over a century ago.

50 ml/2 oz. VSOP Cognac

10 drops of Angostura bitters

ginger ale, to top up

long lemon twist, to garnish

Prepare a tall glass with the garnish of a long
twist of lemon. Fill with ice cubes and add the
ingredients; then stir.

MIX IT UP

Replacing the traditional large lemon twist
garnish with a twist of orange zest will add a
subtle difference in flavour to this old-timer.

SIDECAR

The Sidecar, like many of the classic cocktails created in the 1920s, is attributed to the inventive genius of Harry McElhone, who founded Harry's New York Bar in Paris. It is said to have been created in honour of an eccentric military man who would roll up outside the bar in the sidecar of his chauffeur-driven motorcycle.

50 ml/2 oz. brandy

20 ml/⅔ oz. fresh lemon juice

20 ml/⅔ oz. Cointreau

sugar, for the glass

Shake all the ingredients together over ice and strain into a chilled martini glass with a sugared edge.

MIX IT UP

Try a subtle switch to prevent messing with this classic too much: replace the regular brandy with calvados to create a sophisticated Apple Sidecar.

APRICOT ROYALE _{pictured opposite}

Serve this one to guests who need a bit of livening up! The fruity melody of flavours combines with the Champagne to make this drink the perfect cure for the blues.

50 ml/2 oz. apricot brandy

20 ml/⅔ oz. fresh lemon juice

20 ml/⅔ oz. sugar syrup (page 91)

a dash of peach bitters

a dash of orange bitters

Champagne, to float

apricot slice, to garnish

Add all the ingredients, except the Champagne, to a shaker filled with ice, shake sharply and strain into a rocks glass filled with ice.

Gently layer a float of Champagne over the surface of the drink. Garnish with an apricot slice and serve.

BLOOD & SAND

This cocktail is an example of how a drink should never be judged by anything less than the sum of its parts. It should taste like your favourite festive pudding.

25 ml/1 oz. Scotch whisky

25 ml/1 oz. sweet vermouth

25 ml/1 oz. cherry brandy

25 ml/1 oz. orange juice

Add all the ingredients to a shaker filled with ice, shake sharply then strain into a frosted martini glass.

PISCO SOUR

Pisco is a type of brandy produced in Peru and Chile. It's so popular in its native Peru that there is actually a 'national pisco day'. This cocktail is a shining example of how a cocktail can bring an underappreciated spirit to light.

50 ml/2 oz. pisco

25 ml/1 oz. fresh lemon juice

15 ml/½ oz. sugar syrup (page 91)

15 ml/½ oz. egg white

2 dashes of Angostura bitters

Add all the ingredients to a shaker filled with ice. Shake sharply and strain into a Champagne flute.

SOUR ITALIAN pictured opposite

25 ml/1 oz. Campari

15 ml/½ oz. Strega

15 ml/½ oz. Galliano

25 ml/1 oz. fresh lemon juice

15 ml/½ oz. cranberry juice

15 ml/½ oz. sugar syrup (page 91)

a dash of egg white

2 dashes of Angostura bitters

A cocktail made completely from Italian ingredients, the Sour Italian makes a delicious aperitif.

Shake all the ingredients over ice and strain into a chilled Champagne flute.

BLUEBERRY AMARETTO SOUR

pictured opposite

If you want to add that special touch to a cocktail and don't mind putting in a bit of work, then this is well worth the effort.

50 ml/2 oz. blueberry-infused amaretto*

25 ml/1 oz. fresh lemon juice

15 ml/½ oz. sugar syrup (page 91)

Add all the ingredients to a shaker filled with ice, shake sharply and strain into a pre-chilled liqueur glass.

*Blueberry-infused amaretto: Pierce ten blueberries with a knife and place them in a bottle of amaretto. Leave them to infuse for a few days, shaking occasionally, and taste. Pass the mixture through a fine strainer before using it.

MIDORI SOUR

Shake this one hard, go gentle on the sugar syrup and you'll have a great-tasting, balanced and dramatic-looking cocktail.

50 ml/2 oz. Midori

25 ml/1 oz. fresh lemon juice

1 barspoon sugar syrup (page 91)

a dash of egg white

lemon wheel, to garnish

Add all the ingredients to a shaker filled with ice, shake sharply and strain into a rocks glass filled with ice. Garnish with a lemon wheel and serve with two short straws (optional).

CAIPIRINHA

Cachaça, a spirit indigenous to Brazil, is distilled directly from the juice of sugar cane. The Caipirinha has made cachaça popular in many countries.

1 lime

2 brown sugar cubes

50 ml/2 oz. cachaça

sugar syrup, to taste
(page 91)

Cut the lime into eighths, squeeze and place in an old-fashioned glass with the sugar cubes, then pound well with a pestle.

Fill the glass with crushed ice and add the cachaça. Stir vigorously and add sugar syrup, to taste. Serve with two straws (optional).

MIX IT UP

Cachaça actually makes a great base for a Bloody Mary in place of vodka, adding a bit of bite to the classic hangover cure. Make a Bloody Caipirinha by referring to the rest of the ingredients and method on page 37.

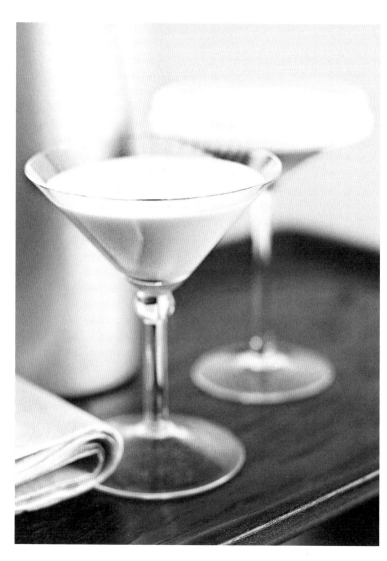

GRASSHOPPER pictured opposite, left

A combination of peppermint and cream, the Grasshopper is the perfect drink to accompany your after-dinner coffee.

25 ml/1 oz. white crème de menthe

15 ml/½ oz. crème de menthe

25 ml/1 oz. single/light cream

Shake all the ingredients over ice, strain into a frosted martini glass and serve.

GOLDEN CADILLAC pictured opposite, right

You could be excused for raising your eyebrows at the mixture of crème de cacao with orange juice and Galliano (herb and liquorice flavoured). If this is too complicated for you, try substituting the crème de cacao with Cointreau.

25 ml/1 oz. white crème de cacao

25 ml/1 oz. single/light cream

50 ml/2 oz. orange juice

a dash of Galliano

Shake all the ingredients over ice, strain into a martini glass and serve.

BRANDY, LIQUEURS & APERITIFS 137

GREEN LADY

The Asian angle in this recipe comes from the juice of the yuzu, a citrus fruit grown in Japan, which has a distinctive flavour described by some people as a cross between mandarin and grapefruit, though others think it's more like a synthesis of lime and grapefruit. A subtle difference! See what you think when you try it.

1 egg white

40 ml/1½ oz. Calvados

15 ml/½ oz. yuzu juice

20ml/⅔ oz. sugar syrup (page 91)

1 barspoon absinthe

1 barspoon matcha green-tea powder

a dash of apple juice

apple slice with a drop of bitters on it, to garnish

Put the egg white in a shaker and stir to break it down (the egg white gives a lovely, rounded, silky texture to the cocktail). Add the rest of the ingredients and ice. Shake, then strain into a glass. Garnish with the slice of apple.

MIX IT UP

Bottled yuzu juice can be found at speciality food stores and Asian markets. If you can't get your hands on the yuzu juice for this recipe, replace with a mixture of 1 part grapefruit to 3 parts lime juice to create a similar flavour. Alternatively, simply use more apple juice for a sweeter finish.

ORANGE BRÛLÉE

pictured opposite

**The Orange Brûlée is a dessert drink that should be savoured.
The only part missing is the blowtorch finish.**

25 ml/1 oz. Grand Marnier

15 ml/½ oz. amaretto

a dash of white crème de cacao

whipping cream, to top

orange zest, to garnish

Add all the ingredients, except the cream, to a shaker filled with ice, shake sharply then strain into a martini glass.

Whip the cream and dollop gently over the surface of the drink. Criss-cross with thin strips of orange zest.

LEMON MERINGUE

Mixing citrus fruits with cream liqueurs generally isn't recommended for cocktails, but somehow this concoction resists the temptation to curdle. It is simply delicious!

50 ml/2 oz. Cytrynowka vodka

20 ml/⅔ oz. lemon juice

15 ml/½ oz. Drambuie Cream

a dash of sugar syrup (page 91)

Add all the ingredients to a shaker filled with ice, shake sharply then strain into a frosted martini glass.

BRANDY ALEXANDER pictured opposite

The perfect after-dinner cocktail, luscious and seductive (and great for all chocolate lovers). It's important, though, to get the proportions right so that the brandy stands out as the major investor.

50 ml/2 oz. brandy

15 ml/½ oz. crème de cacao (dark or white)

15 ml/½ oz. double/heavy cream

nutmeg, to garnish

Shake all the ingredients over ice and strain into a frosted martini glass. Garnish with a sprinkle of nutmeg.

STINGER

A great palate cleanser and digestif which, like brandy, should be consumed after dinner. The amount of crème de menthe used depends on personal taste.

50 ml/2 oz. brandy

25 ml/1 oz. white crème de menthe

Shake the ingredients together over ice and strain into a frosted martini glass.

LEMON DROP

There are various ways to present this sharp shooter. You can coat a lemon slice in sugar and lay it over the surface of the glass to bite into after the shot, or you can take it one step further and soak the lemon slice in Cointreau before coating it, then set it alight!

50 ml/2 oz. lemon vodka

15 ml/½ oz. Cointreau

20 ml/⅔ oz. fresh lemon juice

lemon slice, to garnish

Add all the ingredients to a shaker filled with ice. Shake very hard and strain into a shot glass. Garnish with a lemon slice.

MIX IT UP

Adding half a teaspoon of lemon sherbet powder to the shaker will really give this drink an extra sparkle. Don't add too much or the consistency will be too foamy to drink in shot form. Alternatively, lace the rim of the shot glass with the sherbet.

PURPLE HAZE

The Purple Haze is a classic Kamikaze with a twist – a drink
that belies its strength and will kick-start any evening's fun.
Let the good times roll!

1 white sugar cube

½ lime

50 ml/2 oz. vodka

a dash of Grand Marnier

25 ml/1 oz. Chambord

Put a sugar cube and the fresh lime half, cut into
quarters, into a shaker and crush them together
with a muddler or barspoon. Add the vodka and
Grand Marnier.

Fill the shaker with ice, then shake and strain the
mixture into a chilled shot glass. Float a single
measure of Chambord on to the drink and serve.

MIX IT UP

Take things back to basics by using just 50 ml/
2 oz. vodka, 25 ml/1 oz. triple sec and the juice of
half a lime to make a classic Kamikaze shooter.

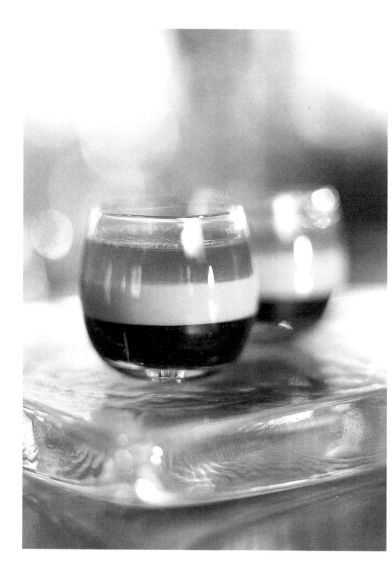

B52

The B52 has reached the lofty peak of being regarded a classic within the world of layered drinks. This shot is best drunk after dinner, as it has a tendency to take the palate by storm.

15 ml/½ oz. Kahlúa
15 ml/½ oz. Baileys
15 ml/½ oz. Grand Marnier

Layer each ingredient on top of each other over a barspoon in a shot glass.

MIX IT UP
You are spoilt for choice with the variations that can be had with a B52. For a B51 replace the Grand Marnier with Frangelico, for a B53 replace with vodka and for a B54 replace with tequila. You can keep going until you have exhausted all the spirits!

PIMM'S CUP

pictured opposite, right

The perfect summer cooler, this cocktail benefits from the addition of elaborate fruit salad-type garnishes. Surprisingly, the tastiest addition to this drink is the cucumber, but strawberries are also an absolute winner. One fruit addition that doesn't really work is lime – the strong citrus juice is too overwhelming.

50 ml/2 oz. Pimm's No 1

250 ml/1 cup lemonade/
lemon soda

75 ml/3 oz. ginger beer

cucumber slice

lemon slice

orange slice

fresh strawberry

fresh mint sprig

Build all the ingredients in a highball glass filled with ice. Stir gently and serve with two straws.

MIX IT UP
For a festive variation try making the Pimm's Winter Cup with the brandy-based Pimm's No 3, apple juice and sliced apples and oranges to garnish.

also pictured: Horse's Neck (see page 125 for recipe)

CHAMPAGNE
& WINE

BELLINI
pictured opposite

The stylish Bellini originated in Harry's Bar in Venice in the early 1940s.

½ fresh peach, blanched

15 ml/½ oz. crème de pêche

a dash of peach bitters (optional)

Champagne, to top up

peach ball, to garnish

a blender

Purée the peach in a blender and add to a Champagne flute. Pour in the crème de pêche and the peach bitters, and gently top up with Champagne, stirring carefully and continuously. Garnish with a peach ball in the bottom of the glass, then serve.

AL FRESCO BELLINI

A quick stir and the colourful stripes in this drink meld into a gentle, magical hue.

20 ml/⅔ oz. peach purée

15 ml/½ oz. Apérol liqueur

Champagne, chilled, to top up

Chinese gooseberry and a rose petal, to garnish

Create three layers by gently pouring into the glass each ingredient in turn over the flatter end of a long, double-ended barspoon: first the peach purée, then the Apérol, followed by the Champagne. Garnish with the Chinese gooseberry and rose petal.

When the cocktail is ready to serve and is in front of the drinker, stir.

KIR ROYALE

After a shaky start, the Kir Royale is now the epitome of chic
sophistication. It started life as the Kir, which contained acidic
white wine instead of Champagne, and was labelled rinse
cochon (French for 'pig rinse'). Luckily, the wine became less
sharp and the drink adopted a more appropriate mantle.

a dash of crème de cassis

Champagne, to top up

Add a small dash of crème de cassis to a
Champagne flute and gently top up with
Champagne. Stir gently and serve.

MIX IT UP

For an original Kir use a good quality white wine
instead of Champagne. A more unusual variation
is a Kir Pamplemousse, made with red grapefruit
liqueur as the base and topped up with sparkling
white wine.

ROSSINI pictured opposite

A great variation on the Bellini, the Rossini can be spiced up with a little Chambord and a dash of orange bitters – two of a bartender's favourite ingredients.

15 ml/½ oz. raspberry purée

1 barspoon Chambord (optional)

2 dashes of orange bitters

Champagne, to top up

Add the purée, Chambord (if using) and bitters to a Champagne flute and top gently with Champagne. Stir gently and serve.

MIMOSA

It is thought that Alfred Hitchcock invented this drink sometime in the 1940s in an old San Francisco eatery called Jack's for a group of friends suffering from hangovers.

½ glass Champagne

2 barspoons Grand Marnier

fresh orange juice, to top up

Pour the orange juice over the Champagne and Grand Marnier and stir gently.

PEACH BLOSSOM SPRING

This is a slight deviation from a classic Bellini, adding a little extra kick with the vodka and peach liqueur. Perfect for serving on a summer's evening or before a dinner party to get the night's proceedings off to a sophisticated start.

25 ml/1 oz. vodka

25 ml/1 oz. peach purée

2 barspoons crème de pêche

prosecco, to top up

2 dashes peach bitters

peach slice, to garnish

Add the vodka, peach purée and crème de pêche to a cocktail shaker filled with ice and shake to mix.

Strain into a Champagne flute and top up with prosecco. Add two dashes of peach bitters and serve garnished with a fresh peach slice.

MIX IT UP

A Lychee Blossom Spring is equally as delicious and great for a tropical-themed evening. Simply use a lychee purée and Liqueur de Lychees with orange bitters. Garnish with a fresh whole lychee on a toothpick.

GINGER CHAMPAGNE

The Ginger Champagne, highly recommended to all sushi lovers, uses an addition of vodka to boost its strength. The ginger combines conspiratorially with the Champagne to create a cocktail that is delicate yet different enough to appease even the most sophisticated of cocktail drinkers.

2 thin slices ginger

25 ml/1 oz. vodka

Champagne, to top up

Put the ginger in a shaker and press with a barspoon or muddler to release the flavour. Add ice and the vodka, shake and strain into a Champagne flute. Top with Champagne and serve.

MIX IT UP

Fire up the ginger element by replacing the vodka with 1 shot of ginger liqueur. Not for the faint hearted.

LIMONCELLO CHAMPAGNE

A fun, refreshing drink to kick off cocktail hour. Great to serve at parties as it is simple and fuss-free.

25 ml/1 oz. limoncello

Champagne, to top up

**FOR THE LIMONCELLO
(MAKES 1 LITRE/4½ CUPS)**

12 Meyer lemons

750 ml/3¼ cups vodka

200 g/1 cup caster/
  granulated sugar

350 ml/1½ cups water

*a large sterilized glass jar
  and sterilized bottles with
  airtight lids*

Pour a splash of limoncello in the bottom of a chilled Champagne glass and top with the Champagne. Serve at once.

LIMONCELLO

Making your own limoncello for this cocktail is easy and rewarding. Peel the lemons, avoiding the pith. Juice the lemons into a sterile glass jar and add the peeled zest. Pour in the vodka and stir. Cover and set aside at room temperature for 2 weeks.

Make sugar syrup: bring the sugar and water to a boil in a saucepan over a medium–high heat. Reduce the heat and simmer for 10 minutes, stirring occasionally until the sugar has dissolved. Remove from the heat and allow to cool.

Add the syrup to the Limoncello mixture and set aside for 30 minutes. Strain the liqueur through a muslin/cheesecloth into a jug/pitcher. Decant into sterilized bottles. Store in the refrigerator or freezer for up to 12 months.

FRENCH 75 <small>pictured opposite, left</small>

Named after the big artillery gun from the First World War,
which rattled off rounds at a rate of 30 per minute, this is
a cocktail that will certainly shake you up.

20 ml/⅔ oz. gin

2 barspoons fresh
lemon juice

1 barspoon sugar syrup
(page 91)

Champagne, to top up

lemon zest, to garnish

Shake the gin, lemon juice and sugar syrup over
ice and strain into a Champagne flute. Top with
Champagne and garnish with a long strip of
lemon zest.

JAMES BOND <small>pictured opposite, right</small>

The naming of this cocktail is a mystery, since the eponymous
spy liked his drinks shaken not stirred, as in this cocktail.
Could be because it's just incredibly suave.

1 white sugar cube

2 dashes of Angostura bitters

25 ml/1 oz. vodka

Champagne, to top up

Place the sugar cube in a Champagne flute and
moisten with 2 dashes of Angostura bitters. Add
the vodka and top up with Champagne.

ELIXIR

Kammerling's Ginseng Spirit is made up of over 45 different botanicals, which is probably why the character of this cocktail has as an 'apothecary' nuance – hence the name Elixir.

20 ml/⅔ oz. Kammerling's Ginseng Spirit

20 ml/⅔ oz. sugar syrup (page 91)

25 ml/1 oz. jasmine pearl tea

150 ml/5 oz. Champagne

fresh violets, to garnish

Combine all the ingredients in a shaker. Top up with ice. Stir very gently and very briefly – this 'freshens' and cools the Champagne with the ice, whilst ensuring that it is evenly distributed.

Strain into a Champagne flute. Garnish with the fresh violets.

MIX IT UP

For a variation that is also botanically blissful, use a rose- or violet-flavoured vodka in place of the ginseng spirit.

BLACK VELVET

It is doubtful whether there is another drink in the world that looks more tempting and drinkable than a Black Velvet. Pour it gently into the glass to allow for the somewhat unpredictable nature of both the Guinness and the Champagne.

½ glass Guinness

Champagne, to top up

Half-fill a Champagne flute with Guinness, gently top up with Champagne, and serve.

MIX IT UP

For those of us who can't always afford Champagne, cider can be used instead to make a 'Poor Man's Black Velvet'. Unlike the traditional Black Velvet, however, these two ingredients do not blend well, and you will end up with a layered drink.

SANGRIA CLASSIC pictured opposite

1 bottle dry red wine

150 ml/⅔ cup Grand Marnier

250 ml/1 cup orange juice

50 ml/2 oz. sugar syrup
  (page 91)

3 dashes of Angostura bitters

seasonal fresh fruit,
  to garnish

It's essential know how to make a Sangria. The good news is that there are few rules, so long as you add red wine and fruit. This recipe makes enough to fill a jug/pitcher.

Add all the ingredients to a jug/pitcher filled with ice and stir gently to mix. Serve in ice-filled glasses, garnished with seasonal fruit.

For a special occasion, add a bottle of Champagne to the punch bowl to give it extra fizz.

SANGRIA BLANCO

1 bottle crisp dry white wine

100 ml/⅓ cup elderflower
  liqueur

100 ml/⅓ cup dry vermouth

100 ml/⅓ cup Cointreau

75 ml/3 oz. fresh lemon juice
  (about 2 lemons)

generous 30 ml/1 oz. sugar
  syrup (page 91)

2 heavy dashes of grapefruit
  bitters

seasonal fresh fruit,
  to garnish

The elderflower liqueur adds a wonderful floral note to this classic summer drink and brings out the sweetness of the season's fruits. This recipe makes enough to fill a large jug/pitcher.

Add all the ingredients to a jug/pitcher filled with ice and stir gently to mix. Serve in ice-filled glasses, garnished with seasonal fruit.

MULLED WINE

Traditionally made with red wine, sugar and spices, this drink is always served hot. Try not to let your mixture boil when you heat it as this may impair the flavour. This recipe makes enough to serve 10 people.

2 bottles red wine

100 ml/⅓ cup brandy

pared zest and freshly squeezed juice of 2 clementines

pared zest of 1 lime

pared zest of 1 lemon

200 g/1 cup caster/superfine sugar

1 cinnamon stick

4 cloves

4 pinches of grated nutmeg

1 split vanilla pod/bean

lemon zest and cinnamon sticks, to garnish

Add all the ingredients to a large saucepan set over medium heat. Simmer gently for about 30 minutes, stirring occasionally.

Serve in heatproof glasses garnished with extra lemon zest and cinnamon sticks.

MIX IT UP
Mulled cider is just as delicious to sip on a cold winter's night. Replace the regular brandy with Calvados and add the same spices and fruit to 2 large bottles of good quality cider.

INDEX

RECIPE CREDITS

Recipes by **Ben Reed**, with the following exceptions:

Carol Hilker
Salted Caramel Bourbon
  Milkshake

Elsa Petersen-Schepelern
Ginger Rum
Mint Julep
Watermelon Gin
Whiskey Mac

Janet Sawyer
The Lounger
White Lady with Vanilla

Shelagh Ryan
Best-ever Bloody Mary

Ursula Ferrigno
Mon Cheri
Queen of tarts

Valerie Aikman-Smith
Dark & Stormy
Frozen Peach Margarita
Limoncello Champagne

William Yeoward
Al Fresco Bellini
Almond Vodka Espresso
Apple Martini

Caramel Rob Roy
Classic Martini
Elixir
Green Lady
Horse's Neck
Kentucky
Maple & Walnut Old
  Fashioned
Negroni
Raspberry & Rose Mojito
Whiskey Sour

PICTURE CREDITS

Jan Baldwin
101

Peter Cassidy
85

Jonathan Gregson
5cr, 109

Gavin Kingcome
12, 15, 35, 46, 74, 77, 124, 139, 167

Erin Kunkel
5br, 102, 163

William Lingwood
1, 3, 5bl, 5ar, 6, 9, 11, 16, 19, 25, 27, 31, 32, 38–45, 49, 54, 57, 62–70, 78, 81, 82, 86, 89, 93, 94, 97, 98, 105, 106, 110–114, 118, 121, 122, 127, 128, 131–136, 140–160, 164, 168, 171, 172

James Merrell
58, 73

Gareth Morgans
5cl, 5al, 20, 23, 28, 50, 53, 117

Steve Painter
2, 61, 90

Kate Whitaker
36